Unashamed Observations

A Collection of Prose Poems

by

Richard Krause

For information contact:
Unsolicited Press
Portland, Oregon
www.unsolicitedpress.com
orders@unsolicitedpress.com
619–354–8005

Cover Image: Dan Stone
Cover Design: Kathryn Gerhardt
Editor: Summer Stewart

ISBN: 978-1-963115-18-5

Also by Richard Krause

Blind Insights Into the Writing Process

Crawl Space & Other Stories of Limited Maneuverability

Eye Exams

The Horror of the Ordinary

Optical Biases

Studies in Insignificance

Acknowledgements

These poems first appeared in the following magazines:

"Standing at the Sink" (as "Liking, Liking") *Portland Review*

"Politeness," "She Said She Wrote Me a Letter" (as "A Letter") *Aura*

"Those Stories You Hear," "A Little Boy's Balloon," "Horses in the Street" *The American Poetry Review*

"Finger," "The Little Japanese Girl," "Character," "Know Thyself" *Waves*

"Her Hands" (as "Hands") *Ellipsis*

"The Hand," "Refills," "Candy," "I Often Try to Freeze Faces," "What Happens When You Don't Read?" *FragLit*

"Respect for Books" (as "Books") *qarrtsiluni*

"Irving" *Scapegoat Review*

"Vermont Winter" *Turk's Head Review*

"People Pry," "The Tea Ceremony," "Talent" *Courtship of Winds*

"Nails," "An Ugly Sounding Name" *Offcourse*

"The Hand," "Books That Correspond to the Memory" *Poesis*

"Birds in Cages" *Shot Glass Journal*

"Insight into Myself" *Poemeleon*

"An Amputee" *Triggerfish Critical Review*

"Teeth" *Menacing Hedge*

"A Split Mind Is Convenient to Hide the Axe" *The Five-Two*

I wish to thank S.R. Stewart for selecting this collection

Table of Contents

9

Unashamed Observations

1

On the Bus

Yesterday on the bus, while I was quickly searching my pockets for the change I had misplaced, and the bus was fast approaching my stop, what seemed to be a short fat boy left his seat and bulled into me to get past. It seemed intentional. I then, before I had even found the change in my pockets, stepped forward onto his foot, crushing it with that half-inadvertence that tries to better position itself for a departure. Even before I found my money, so intent was I on getting him back. Both of us, I felt, knew that what I had done was not unintentional. Finally, I found my money just before the bus pulled up to the stop. He got off first and I strode past him only to find that we both were going to cross the street at the same time. It was then that we caught each other's eye simultaneously. He stood at an angle. He was short, stocky, and had a military cap on. Rather older looking than a student, but dressed like one. He then limped across the street almost forgetting me--he was crippled. I didn't know what to think of having crushed his foot so decisively. Only, was it the good one I had stepped on, or the lame foot?

The Orange

Repeatedly I sunk the knife into the orange as it rolled across the table further and further away from me the more I stabbed it. The juice rose in beads each time I withdrew the knife, and gradually left a trail anyone could follow to the orange. Its pulp soon collapsed and left only the torn rind on the table. The skin had indeed merged with the flesh; the sacs seem all to have been broken open and unable to give the torn orange the structure it had before. It was an abortion of an orange. A piece of fruit miscast. A miscarriage. It no longer looked like an orange, but like something that had suffered repeated collisions and released the vital juices beneath it with no longer a desire to function as anything identifiable. Disgusted with having so distorted the orange, with having changed its identity, I cocked my head and as best I could licked up the trail of juice it made on the table. What were the orange live could be called wiping up the trail of fear that it had left behind.

The Hemophiliac

The hemophiliac walk through the world is a constant series of dangers. Projecting points, tables' edges, the snaps on women's dresses, sheets of paper, blades of grass. The very ground he walks on in a moment he could be tumbling towards. The softest earth that seems to hold no danger in a moment will trip him and exact the libation it desires. The ground, having passed the day when portions of it were consecrated, exacts its rights from the hemophiliac, the easy mark who in an instant will spill blood for it. And how many years will one track of land wait for the hemophiliac, how many bunches of flowers will it support, and how much practice will it get absorbing rainfall? And how it will finally disdain it as not the real thing. All the time waiting for drops of blood that are no longer poured willingly on it, but that it must trip the hemophiliac up for.

Politeness

He was very polite. As a matter of fact he asked me in the best English if he could smoke. Of course, I said yes, but looked away shyly and embarrassed. At his English, because of his politeness, I don't know from what. But why did I then look down at his foot, out of the corner of my eye, and imagine I saw his shoe off and only his gray stocking? The thought of this rudeness--without even asking--this impoliteness irritated me. I wanted to show my displeasure, though as before I could hardly look at his feet for fear of arousing my indignation even further. I then thought of swinging my boot down past the gray folds of his trousers onto his unprotected foot. Pretending simply to be finding a more relaxed position for my crossed legs, when just before that I noticed to my surprise that his shoe was not off, but that it had been tucked under his seat just enough that with the support of his matching folds of pants I had gotten the impression that his shoe was off. I then realized that I had wanted to see his shoe off, to take offense at him for the politeness he had trapped me into.

An Amputee

An amputee, sitting next to me on the train, keeps a one arm vigilance over his stump. Though I steal a glance at it, it is not long enough to allow it to sprout in my imagination either a hand or the missing fingers. I am always intrigued by missing body parts--intrigued over their place of absence. Now he's covering up the stump with a magazine, a cheap magazine. I wonder who chopped off his hand. And for what reason--stealing? Merciless thought. But no mercy can put the hand back on. So why not? It is a godless loss, and no god can restore it. But why doesn't he have prosthetics done? But then what of my natural impressions, what would that artificiality do to them? Do you suppose he had me in mind when he didn't have the work done? Maybe my response that he's feeling now is a deterrent to such restorative thoughts. And maybe he keeps it unclad, exiting pinkly and swallowed (it looks as if the skin is swallowing itself), just to stir my imagination. Droll thought, but that is not all! What if I just reached over and kissed it! Do you think the moisture of my lips would animate it, make it grow fingers that would reach into my mouth for my tongue and pull on it admiringly as a lifesaver? A no more repugnant idea could occur to me. And that is just why I think it. There he's covered up his arm again. Earlier he tried smoking, and now he's stopped after I coughed in my throat--a forced cough--he put it out half-lit. He must have some feelings. I imagine a relationship between us. Perhaps a friendship over his handlessness. What an intimate basis for friendship to take hold, where my thoughts grasp what his body can't handle. Now he's pulled his sleeve down and is leaning over it with his free arm. He's playing the maiden, I can tell, but this time I look the other way.

Hand

I mistakenly said, "You have a large hand." His reply was, "No, I don't think so." Then putting his hand up to have mine join it in measurement, I was forced to make contact with him. (I quickly realized my mistake.) Feeling his cold clammy skin against mine, chills raced down my spine, all I wanted to do was wash my hand as soon as possible. I held it under the table, apart from the rest of my body, not letting it touch it until I had an excuse to leave him--the coldness, the clamminess stayed with me, clung to me. What is the reason I was so revolted by this simple contact with a fellow human being? I don't think I inspire the same kind of abomination in him; in fact, he was eager for such contact. And why should his skin be any different than mine, any more loathsome, abominable? Is it because he is unattractive, or wears thick glasses, or is not a woman? And it is not something I can control, I have no bad thoughts or opinions of him--it has nothing to do with anything intellectual or thought out--it is purely tactile, in the skin itself. But how is it that I know the injustice, the unfairness of this, and still can remain feeling unjust or unfair? Because there are injustices beyond our control. That we must live with and abide in ourselves, even though they contradict what is otherwise our moral nature. We try to be good and fair, but our skin--against our will--crawls with an opposite intention.

Finger

I showed her the bump on my writing finger. And then she showed me her finger--the little one had been sliced off at the tip and rested back on healed, but a fraction of a centimeter off center. In other words, the part severed, not much larger than the small finger's fingerprint. In fact, that portion with a little more reaching up to the nail. The portion of a little child's hand that you'd imagine was probably reaching somewhere dangerous, inquisitively, thoughtlessly placing itself in a position to get sliced clean off. She who had grown up to work a scissors, cut hair, now stretched out her fingers to show me. I half-looked, thinking almost simultaneously--I was amazed at myself--why did you go and do that? Don't you know what kind of person I am--that even though I am attracted to you I can't help myself. But a fingerprint displaced would ruin your identity for me. I mean, it's not down on all five like a normal set. Now it is drifting up--permanently--towards the original torment of the cut. I still hear the cry in that little finger that some twenty years later you feel compelled to show a stranger you've just met a few hours ago, a stranger whose mind is as mercilessly sharp as the blade that cut the finger in the first place. Who recreates the childhood scene in his mind. In whose mind just like in your own the pain, the moment won't now rest. Already he has woken up the next morning thinking about it. It was the first thing on his mind. And now this, what he's writing. A word of warning: next time don't show your finger to a stranger. Or if it is someone you care about, wait until he is in your grip before you are so careless with your hands again.

Her Hands

She was always having trouble with her hands. The cracked dry palms, the creases at the fingers, would separate down to the bloodline with deep fissures. I'd find her at the lamp with a needle and a magnifying glass, puncturing the tiniest blisters and pustules that were invisible to the naked eye. For hours she would be at her hands, poking the microscopic blisters that as often as not rose in response to her own needle. Physicians had no idea about the cracking, all known funguses were ruled out; it seemed to be just a case of the spontaneous eruption of the skin in response to the companionless life she led, to her living by herself for so long; it was only natural that the hands swelled, grew red and sensitive, were poked with needles--you could see her under the lampshade even when you visited still giving pleasure to herself, hearing the exclamations of "ooh" and "ahh" when the needle penetrated her skin. Yes, pleasure at the companionship of the needle all steely and sharp penetrating her skin, exposing tiny blisters that ran with a clear fluid that awarded her with the pleasure of having burst another pustule. She showed you this under the magnifying glass with a sense of triumph, like it was a reward almost. The ointments, the salves, the cotton and gauze that she wrapped her hands in before sleep, the emollients all gave her a sense of accomplishment. But you could tell she took more pleasure from the long drafts of air she inhaled to convey to you that they hurt, were cracking again, fissuring, even the thenar region had little scarifying nicks. The only portions that were saved were the palmistry lines, the life, the head, the heart lines. It was as if something in her body refused their obliteration. That the dryness, the redness, the crusting of the rest of the hand (especially between the fingers where the itchiness was unbearable, she said) almost made it a cake of some unearthly dirt masquerading as something other than a hand didn't matter; the lifeline was for the most part intact, the head knew what it was doing angling the needle into her skin, the heart too, responded by bleeding at the appropriate times. How she could still be so absorbed in her hands when I was there I didn't know till I realized that she needed spectators to view how she overcame her loneliness even in their presence, that even with so much cracking, scabbing, with such deep fissures, and with what must have been genuine pain, even despite the mystery as to the etiology, the actual cause of the fungus, she wanted to demonstrate--and even with the absence of a companion--to demonstrate that her life was still--despite their ravaged condition--still in her own hands.

The Hand

The hand, and what it holds, holds my attention. An empty hand also holds my attention. I watch to see what it does with itself. What it does with its emptiness. Rarely does it stay empty. It always holds onto something. To its other hand, to its own body, to a table, to a pencil, or it curls up into a half-fist, or clenches itself full-fisted. I am not sure how I want the hand to be. Open-palmed? Isn't it then about to grasp something? And most vulnerably? Even our hand cannot be alone. It is the best sign of us.

One Japanese Man

One Japanese man on one side of the train talks forcefully to the four sitting across from him, emphasizing his clipped sentences by moving his fist up and down. The four look unconvinced, so that even by the time he has unclenched his fist, they are already stealing glances at each other. Now they have started to talk back, cautiously at first, then to fall silent again. Suddenly, whether from their inattention, or because he senses his own inability to convince them of the things he says, he pushes up his sleeve, takes a long hatpin out of his wallet, and sticks it in his crooked arm right up to the bead he is holding it with. "There, and there, there, and there," he says. 'Do you believe me now?" But perhaps because of the slenderness of the pin, or the muscularity of the arm, there isn't even the tiniest rill of blood. As he pulls the pin out the flesh seems to close each time. Still the four look at each other, then away, unconvinced of the man's added demonstration of his argument.

The Little Japanese Girl

The little Japanese girl repeatedly throws her body against the fence I am leaning on in the only way she knows to communicate with me. I feel the exclamations, the questions, the periods of the sentences she would want to ask if she could express herself with anything less than her whole body.

The Tea Ceremony

It has just occurred to me that making love is just the opposite of the tea ceremony. Or if they were to be considered the same, the cups would have to be snatched out of the participants' hands and shattered on those large stones found outside the tea room in Japanese gardens. The hot tea would be spattered over the colorful kimonos. The server would have her powdered tea container upset in a small cloud of green dust. The bamboo whisk brush would fall on the tatami and roll in the corner. The hanging scroll over the small alcove would be pulled down in the effort to get hold of the kimono. Everyone else would have fled. Finally, you'd unloosen the obi and undrape the kimono, and after completely undoing the long swirls of the most colorful material, you would have overcome the idea of diametrical opposites, and merged the tea ceremony with lovemaking.

2

Talent

To have talent that spills over every effort. That you are surfeited on every side. That every turning wastes. What to do? The less prudent build reservoirs, try to contain. Their talent stagnates behind genres, has lines drawn around it like roast beef, has the fleet foot bound. The overabundance achieves rhyme hobbling. Achieves beat. What runs fluid and free is put in a watercourse. Locked in chapters, or harnessed in scenes it wears like a bridle, or worse--an oxbow around the neck. The talent ceases to course, the mane no longer trails in the wind. The elflocks on the feet no longer trail in freedom. They are clipped not to interfere with the heaviest of shoes--work shoes. Not to create anew, but to furrow and deepen what is. To plant, reap, and sow. It is the animal husbandry of talent. The farming of it out of the wilds, finally the marketing of it, that sells.

A Story Later

In an hour, a story later, you change the complexion of the day. Most days have a bad complexion. You apply the creams of short work, massage the individual pores, but they rarely have the lasting effect of a long piece. But even that is not emollient enough, and before you know it, just because you scour your desk for a topic, because of the soaps you've grown accustomed to, the complexion is eczematic again, flaky, and you have to apply the disfiguring ointment zinc oxide. All the creams you try, when work alone (one story) will bring the natural blush you want. You turn on yourself again and again with one liners, and that seems to smooth the surface with the beginning of a grimace, a sneer, but finally it deepens and scores, the line stops permanently on the face, and is added to what you haven't written.

Some Mornings

Some mornings my talent can think anything. It is like an octopus whose tentacles have become as independent as snakes (that collect about my head like a medusa). And though I have the suppleness, the bite to sink my thoughts into anything, though they are sharp and venomous enough, though I can ingest anything I want, in a moment there is too much to my thought. It is a whirl. Twisting and stretching, hissing and sighing, alternately relaxing in the clear languor of a new day and already slithering noiselessly in the brush. My thinking can take no productive turn long enough to clearly and simply produce the furry trot of a rabbit, for example. Nothing like that for my thoughts to untangle enough for at least one of them to fill my writer's stomach with any sense of satisfaction. Or if it does happen, it is always with a rabbit of my own making. And even if I hold it up (by the ears) for observation, my thoughts regard it with suspicion like they would a magician's rabbit as only being a trick, a sleight of hand, and nothing worthy of my thinking to pounce on.

What Happens When You Don't Read?

What happens when you don't read and don't get out? Your work starts to overlap, duplicate itself, multiply incestuously. One piece is lying atop another, in the same bed of thought so to speak, and whatever creaks in one part of the house is picked up in the next. And jealousies ensue, the proud assertions of male dominance, the female wiles, the seductions of your own work trying to outdo, emasculate, reinvigorate itself, but in the end it is all incestuous, all the same family of desires, the weaknesses predominate, the strengths don't outlive the household, there is no fresh blood and the diseases of inbreeding finally win out in work after all that no one else is related to.

Respect for Books

He has an undue respect for books. He never marks them up, or reads while eating, for fear of soiling them. He respects and pays allegiance to all he reads. I tear to shreds the pages in his presence. Mount the most convincing arguments why this or that book should not be read, why my markings in the margins, my underlining, checks, asterisks, why whole paragraphs I've xed out are superior to the printed page that he keeps virgin and unthumbed. I tell him nothing will grow in the forest of books you have, the three books you read a week. You've got to take your pen to them, scarify them, tear, shred the pages. Your mind should be like a lumber mill. It should spin with the sharp weight of gears, sprockets with the teeth of thought meant to sever and section trees, that's how you should handle pages, as if every book you read were walking the plank.

Books That Correspond to the Memory

The books that correspond to the memory. That conjure up the exact moment. I have a lifetime of them. Could it be that so carefully reading them somehow absorbed the place I was at with the same precision, the same atmosphere? That the book, just by its physical proximity, was like my finger on the trigger, that turning the pages years later set off explosions, associations of time and place that had I not the book in my hand I would never have remembered. It's as if my existence to be remembered needed almost that parallel life in the book, that somehow the book drew into relief the life I was living just because it didn't touch me. Just because the reality, though nestled in my own, was very different from it. Nevertheless, the book in my hand was almost a prayer that made sacred where I was. Consecrated the time and place to memory. With her, e.g., just off the top of my head I can name twenty books and just what she was doing then, how she occupied herself as I read.

The Bookworm

The bookworm devours what he reads, leaving the book vermiculate. That after you open it, you can tell only its cover. In other words, you can tell just through what letters the worm has tunneled. For openers the "o"s that he favored first. The easy access they gave. Then you go on to the other letters and find the bookworm distorted what he read randomly, just to devour it. Finally, you conclude that indeed though he is a so-called bookworm, he is unlettered.

Choice Cuts of Wit

Here a few choice cuts of wit. The hide too, the horns that butt, the transparent eye that the reader will see himself in. The hock, the hooves, the unusable portions will adhere to the mind like the glue they can be turned into. The open vents of inspiration, the hot air of the nostrils will help the reader breathe more easily. Even imagine a velvet touch to some of the sentences that will give his own hand a warm pleasure for what he himself hasn't created, but feels a power quicken from contact with what I've done. It is the cattle in me that will be noticed, the full udder that will make the flow of feeling productive. And the tail end, the wisps of thought, perhaps they can be used as a switch when experience itself becomes too irritating--winged. And alights where you don't want it to. Maybe something I've written will slap it off.

Beating a Dead Horse

Going over the same material. It's like beating a dead horse. But of course, there can be consolation in that. If the horse is recently dead. If it still has some sponginess to its muscles, something to bounce off of, something to give you all the satisfaction of resistance, that you are not beating the air, or simply shattering bleached white ribs, working up a desert sweat. No, the horse has to be of recent demise, but not long enough for the flies to have found it, or the flesh to become tainted. For you want the sweet scent of your own perspiration, the body expenditure over allying yourself with those theories of sexuality psychologists attribute to horses. Maybe that, more than anything else, is why you take a club to the horse.

I Write Fast This Morning

I write fast this morning, sensing that I will soon be interrupted. Writing ahead of the noise I will hear. Cacophonous sounds begin to appear in my sentences, ash cans in back alleys, pots and pans rattling in every disgruntled kitchen, fists banging on the tin pan walls of my mind, for the brass, the silver, the gold that doesn't jingle there. Noise always has something to do with our own greed, with coins of truth that drop out of avarice, out of complaining about disturbances outside us to hide the racket our desires, our need and ambitions make on the inside moving the pen across the page as noisily as we can to try to out-sound the disturbance we are to ourselves.

Currents of Thought

There are so many currents of thought, conflicting riptides, that feed often irrelevantly into each other, that it is amazing that the stream of my thinking advances enough to express even one sentence clearly and unroiled. That one doesn't see only, e.g., sinking keels or the mast of a "t" of a sentence that I wanted to say. There's a buoyancy to language that stubbornly remains on the surface of things. A lack of cargo that heavier, more grave talents are shipwrecked by.

What If There Were a Person?

What if there were a person who read only what other people didn't? That once they said, "Oh, I've read him," he felt bound to deny what he read, admit some mistake. Now what if this passed on to knowledge, so that he never made claims to what everyone knew, in fact stubbornly pleaded ignorance? Instead, that what he knew constituted only what others didn't. What he found though was that they were constantly appropriating what he considered his own private knowledge. Even about himself. That finally they encroached so much that he had to admit that no, he didn't know himself just because, yes, they did.

The Notebook Company

The notebook company, responding to the daily increase of inflation, cuts back yearly on the number of pages in the notebooks it sells. One year it has so reduced the pages that it only has paper enough for the covers, thick substantial covers that hide the fact that all the pages are absent. But writers continue to buy the notebooks and pretend to fill the absent pages. They submit the notebooks to publishers, who themselves pinched by inflation, by a paper shortage, pretend that the best work of modern literature is only now at the turn of the century being written. Cocktail parties are held in country estates to herald the arrival of talents that haven't been seen in a hundred years. Meanwhile, outside the windows of such estates, huge trees grow in size for all the paper latent in their bark, for all the actual pages that could have been written.

3

Those Stories You Hear

Like those stories you hear from time to time of those lovers who put their girlfriend's names on billboards, asking them to marry. You wonder after they get over the shock of it, after it wears off and the paper starts to curl, and the letters lose their luster, finally their character, do the feelings too, by that time, come to be replaced by cigarette advertisements, or bourbon commercials? Does the man just because of his initial enthusiasm not take to a similar habit that the billboard generated, and once he is hooked must sustain? Feeding his need after the woman with cigarettes and alcohol. And the woman too, though you'd imagine her sitting in the car, not looking up, not believing him at first, you'd imagine the woman ever after reading the same billboard, and over every change of habit that she too by now shares in hoping for there to be a replay of the time when her name, and his love for her, was similarly advertised.

Horses in the Street

He steps over her almost to position himself on the curb side of the street. And when I criticize him for being old-fashioned, he replies: It's for the imaginary horses. Their galloping there. The golden manes, the flashing hooves. The palomino, the pink underside of the dapple grays. It's for the commotion in the street, the equine life, the trotting, prancing, the chest-high heart reined in by a silver harness, the flower between the ears of the children's ponies, all these things, the life in the street is what I move over and protect her from, at the same time grasping the reins of the past with an imagination that champs on the bit of the present to turn it into a deeper life, more proud of instinct, with all the animal spirits that my walking on the right side will allow. And each time she understands me and never once has questioned my move. Can you understand? Or maybe it is just a hidden desire to mount her. The abashment at this imagines horses in the street.

"He Thought He Was Entitled to More"

"He thought he was entitled to more," she said. She was talking about this Indian she met in Hong Kong who gave her a jar of chutney, and took her to a restaurant. Afterwards she said it was then that he thought there was more coming. "What could that have been?" I said. "I don't quite understand." She smiled at me, a trifle unbelieving. Almost with an arch, mischievous smile that was bursting to show the pixie in her. "You're playing dumb," she finally said, taking a different tack. "I guess I am," I smiled. As if somewhere deep inside I wanted to get retribution for the Indian. Leave an arrow somewhere in her body where he failed to. For some reason his having missed the mark, I as a man wanted to get back at her for him. And beyond that I couldn't explain it myself. Except that I found myself standing up and saying, "Well, I have to go, it's getting late." "Oh, already?" she said, stiffening up and moving away from me. I knew she wanted me to stay. Was willing to give what she thought the Indian she met in Hong Kong wasn't entitled to. But I was at the other end of that refusal. I didn't want what she was willing to give, just because he did when she was unwilling. I felt outside under the stars Emerson's law of compensation. I don't remember if he had a sexual purpose in mind when he formulated it, but here outside I felt the ebb and flow of refusal and acquiescence was better consummated than had I stayed with her the night. (Or maybe it was just the three kinds of rancid cheese that she ate earlier in the evening that turned me off.)

An Ugly Sounding Name

I never liked someone with an ugly sounding name—the *-sawa* at the end of her name (though aptly suffixed and common in Japan) repelled me, while her personal charms attracted me. Nevertheless, the name kept repeating itself in my mind over and over again, insisting that I be disenchanted with her. As if her name alone had an aesthetic life that competed with and wanted to overturn my natural attraction to her. It was as if her name was independently alive, and that no matter what personal preference I had for her, it was bound to be interfered with by the resounding pronunciation of her name within my ears. No matter how much I tried to focus my attention on her separate and individual charms, the name--its suffix alone separated for me into hissings s's, elongating to a painful ahhh! and finally an expressive waaa! that rang with the sense of an unformed question--came between us. And as much as I tried to escape the separateness of her name, detach her from it, the more its latter part cohered with a porcine stubbornness that crowded out whatever delicacy I found on her face, that upturned her nose and emphasized its wrinkling saying it--which I had her do many times to torment myself. Her name selected her most unattractive features, its sound in her mouth made them visual for me each time. The vowelate ease of its repetition (sometimes I imagined she almost took pleasure saying her name for me!) kept misshaping them, warping my desire for her. It pugged the nose unsympathetically, it narrowed the eyes to an unlustered squint, it enlarged the ears driving the chin towards the lips so that it easily assisted the upturned nose in exposing only the nostrils. Finally, I turned away from her face because of her name.

Two Lovers

Two lovers. One goes away to England, leaves her home country, Japan. Comes back bloated and fat. Her face and body are so full she could be floating. She agrees to meet you. Is looking away almost after your eyes meet. The accusation is implicit. Or at least you imagine it is. From non-love. From your letting her go, not meeting her in England as she had suggested. Telling her to forget about you so she'll not be hindered if she meets someone nice. All this she went and ate for. And the accusation is there in the eyes. In the round face fattened around them. Your thinness is threatened by it. The conception you have of your humanity falters. But wait, there's an extenuation! The skinny lover. The one who left and came back thinner. Who exercises three hours a day since she left. She you can be proud of having abandoned. She who you drove into her body. To the warm tropical climate where she could reveal more of it. She who now has no need of you. Does she cancel out the other? Is it possible that the thinness of the one has made up for the fatness of the other? And that the fruits of unlove have resulted in the added weight to one and loss to another. And that finally you can't calculate body weight on the basis of love withheld.

Picture of His Wife in a Kimono

He takes a picture of his wife in a kimono seated across from him on the train. She pretends not to notice, then after he snaps the picture wrinkles her forehead once, and moves her nose just enough so he can see it signaling her part in its completion. He of course, right after snapping the picture, drops his camera case. That's his way of apologizing for having taken the picture in front of us.

Standing at the Sink

She was standing at the sink with her back to me, washing dishes and attending the stove. I put the eggs in the refrigerator one by one, and when I had emptied the plastic carton began, I don't know why, crumpling it in my hands, louder and louder, as if the whole universe were crackling and crumpling, as if it were reduced to one willful, strident noise that only wanted to irritate and nothing else. But she did not move. She kept her back towards me. Again I started crumpling it, this time even more vigorously than before, but she remained fixed with her back towards me. I got up out of the chair and walked towards her, crumpling the plastic egg carton as I approached, and bent close to her as I pushed it into the trash and said, "Doesn't that bother you?" "Yes," she said, "but you like it."

Candy

The little girl sneaks a piece of candy into her mouth. I imagine its sugars dissolving in secret, the crystals breaking down, the saliva activated and excited, rising to the occasion; the cheek sucking on the candy, and the tongue biting itself to get all the pleasure the mouth can out of the surreptitious insertion of the candy. And the beauty of the eyes. They triumphant as they look around to see if anyone has noticed the orgy of pleasure the mouth has experienced, the tongue proclaiming the sweets to the roof of the mouth, drawing every nook of delight into her enjoyment, vacuuming the mouth for the emptiness of her little life unpleased, for the predeterminate stage of her own sexuality that can only be bridged by this hard structure of candy dissolving, breaking down in her mouth by her sucking on it for dear life.

The Laughter of Virgins

Like the laughter of virgins past or passing the age of fertility--all the high-pitched unfulfillment of it. The sheer slopes of it, the fluid precipitates, the glissando play of it, like sunlight on dazzling snow for the body just beneath. For this is its highest moment, this laughter cascading out of it, this detour of white teeth and the broadest grin. This tragedy of unproductivity that can only be coped with by being laughed at. By playing the giddy adolescent whose chances have not already passed.

Her Tears

She showed me her tears just at the point when her eyes were brimful; she knew the exact moment to turn to me just before they would run down her cheeks. I stopped this for good one day when we were at the dinner table by saying, "Fine, now bring your face over my plate. You can salt my potatoes."

A Little Boy's Balloon

The man is writing on the street with a pen. Without looking, he collides with a little boy's balloon. It bursts and the boy looks wide-eyed. Amazed. The man looks all around the crowd to find where the balloon was bought. But not finding that, he does the next best thing. He himself bursts into tears before the little boy, who now stares dry-eyed at the spectacle of a grown man crying in public over a burst balloon.

Waiting

She spots who she's waiting for, smiles and grabs her things. They're off together. This simple, seemingly insignificant gesture to the observer takes on an importance quite exceeding anything it may have for the two who maybe are only going to a movie, or somewhere to amuse themselves. In fact, it is a marvel--the waiting, the anticipation, the arrival, the smile, the grabbing of her things, his reaching out his hand, she giving a little skip as she grabs it. What more is there? Absolutely nothing, except writing about it. And that finally is less.

4

I Often Try to Freeze Faces

I often try to freeze faces, keep my feelings for them unchanged. There is something frozen in my desires, some unthawing principle even when women are flowing towards me, melting in my arms. Something out in the cold that even women closest to me have felt. (And had to quickly get their clothes on for.) Little did they know of the mechanical desire for refrigeration, to keep them physically just the same as my love for them. For so deeply did I want them to remain unchanged that each one I finally froze out of my life. But years after they are all there. Even when the electricity went off, when there was no more artificial refrigeration, in the tundra of my consciousness, under the clear icy brilliance of the steppes they live on. Corpses almost of love that never really melted in me. That my mind is bound to, still beautiful as I pay homage to the image of themselves that they left me behind. As if these cold remnants, this aftermath is the very essence of my feeling. That years before even the warmth of living associations with these women, the exchange of the warmest kisses and intimacies was leading up to. As if that warm birth of feeling was only preliminary to what would last in my mind a lifetime compared to the lovers they would soon take. I would still have them in cold storage, so to speak, like mammoth remains.

People Pry

People pry like awls. What you have to do is seal up your crevices. Not even let the least crack of daylight give them a hint of where they can place their instrument. You remain shut like a clam. And though they get angry and chip your shell, with every ounce of muscle you remain closed. And maybe finally they do gain admission. First by that false opening, the mock fenestration that chips the shell leaving a clear green mesentery. But you refuse to show your internal workings. You leave such a confusion that they don't know your eyes from the proverbial hole in the ground. This angers them, this seeming internal confusion. But you take pride in that false fenestration, that mock window that allows them to see into nothing, but rather reflects them. And even when they pull out their knife and slip the sharpest blade through the crack only the chip gave access to, you remain stubbornly, as triumphantly closed as when they work the knife completely around to sever your taut muscle, sever it so that the shell springs open, and with one or two scrapings you are eviscerated, insides scrambled on the sand, and there is nothing to you for all their efforts. They pick you up with the tip of their knife, examine what they were so intent on opening with their blade, but nothing, still you don't expose the eye you see them with. Still your internal conformation is as much of a mystery as when you were closed tight. Frustrated they take the heel of their boot and stamp you into the sand with their toe pointing upward. People pry like awls. They must. For who else would degrade themselves compared to their remote ancestor the eagle who soars with the mystery he can't understand and drops it from a height he can.

Nails

I noticed my cuticle receding. Lately, it has passed my notice. I have been preoccupied with other, more important things. But its invisibility struck me tonight. There's nothing left of it. My nails are naked, unprotected, unbuffered by that soft layer of transparency covering the small white moons that contrast with the pink of the rest of the nail. They usually have receded when I've submitted them to the inclemency of soap detergents—how they suffered under my mania for cleanliness, but before they always returned. Now they have disappeared altogether. Nothing remains. My nails are a desert. Nothing grows atop of them. They are barren, a glaze. Recently they have started to buckle and show ridges, paths of horny striations that lead to the nail's edge, that serve no purpose but to show a material discontent with the surface they make up. My nails seem to have lost their purpose. The skin has fled them, and they don't even scratch me as they were wont to do. They used to dig deeply into my skin, score it with red wheals that would rise like velvet even before the nails had fully left them. To do homage to what created pain--to the pleasure it mixed in. Yes, my skin has always been half in love with my nails. Their capacity for digging, their insensitivity to what was almost a wholly different condition of matter than themselves, so soft is it by comparison. And how it loved the hardness of the nails, the relief they brought. How the skin even in anticipation of that pleasurable relief would exacerbate itself; how tiny networks of itchiness would make it crawl to touch itself, would make it feel the futility of never truly being allied with itself, and how the nails would itch to get at the swaths of skin with the most urgent summons. The nails sometimes would do their duty so well that they would rub the skin raw, neglect all the signals of pain, but scratch and scratch until it was insensate--until red blood replaced the moisture it lacked, until it lubricated the deserted areas of most need, until it quenched the skin's thirst. Quickly however it dried, but sore and inflamed. For days it couldn't be touched, gotten near. And I wonder if the nails felt less useful at those times when they submitted to functions of mock importance like peeling grapes, or pulling tape, or providing leverage to areas inaccessible. For always they would wait for their natural reunion with the body that gave them birth. Crave to scratch what they grew from, hardened for. But lately that desire has left me. Winter is coming, and my body is growing cold. And even the wool sweaters I wear are no longer able it seems to summon the old lust to my fingertips.

Sweater

She said she couldn't go until she finished the sweater for me. I didn't know how to make her leave, since the gift was the price I was paying for her staying. Though I wanted her to leave, her fingers lingered over each stitch, as she sat looking at me with a smile on her face. You don't quite know what to do with a sweater knitted out of devotion to you. The thoughts that pass through the unreciprocated lover's mind. As she imagines that her gift will ransom your feelings. Finally, she finishes. You try on the sweater. The color, you admit, does go with you, was well-chosen, though the sweater doesn't fit, you both know that. But which by agreement you don't discuss. You don't tell her you feel uncomfortable in it. That you can't wait to get it off. That the arms are too short. You try not to reach to show it to her. "All the girls are knitting sweaters for their boyfriends," she says. She shows you the magazine picture of the model you are supposed to look like. Still the sweater is too tight. It hasn't taken into account the size of your chest (maybe it is the heart she's left out). You feel constricted by it, by her feelings that she has stitched you up in, gotten you to wear. You make the appropriate comments, try not to hurt her feelings. But before you know it are wriggling out of the too tight sweater. Her feelings will never fit you. You suspect she already knows that. The sweater, she must know, was only a symbolic effort. She is trying to give poignancy to what has failed between you. Trying, in this one last futile effort, to bring you around. But you have had to wriggle out of her feelings before. Now they are left on the sofa inside out. Yet you embrace her with all the knowledge that soon she will go for good, with the sweater folded up and stored for next year in a plastic bag. You know you will never wear it. Yet you thank her for the excess yarn she gives you just in case it wears through some place.

Your Heart Is in the Right Place

"At least your heart is in the right place," they said. Well, where could it be? For no matter how much they want to emphasize their own correctness, the heart is never misplaced, somewhere else than where it is. And does this not give rise to a deeper reflection? That the position of the heart is always constant, static. That no matter what good or evil the heart does, it is always in the right place.

A Cloud

As a cloud not only filters or impenetrably refuses light, it also contains light, so much so that it is brighter than anything around it. In the same way a sorrow, e.g., will contain the brilliance of a self-supporting state of happiness just because it is so sorrowful, so gloomy, so cloudy, that it makes itself capable of, the repository for, the highest happiness in the way happiness alone never does.

Propagating the Species

Is it that our whole life we are plagued with not looking like we want? Is this why our desires are so multifaced and involve so many people? Is it no more than the failure to bring our own appearance in line with our desires that creates all the craving? That is the impetus for our propagating the species. That if we looked like we wanted, we would have no need to improve ourselves copulating. There being no dissatisfaction.

Weather

"Whether" always documents my attitude towards the weather. It is either this or that. An inner fluctuation. A decision that is at the mercy of my moods. An inner meteorology that decides on the basis of no firm convictions but shifts in blood currents, body pressures, at the speed of nerve impulses. Weather, yes whether, always involves the thoughts clouding for a moment of clarity, brightening, then going inclement again. Still, whether this or that. It's always a matter of the climate having shifted inside.

Insight into Myself

On my insight into myself: I never claim it directly. It is always partial, biased. It is always the result of my probing elsewhere. "I don't know, I don't know" is the litany I use to find out. This nescience gives me the time, the leisure almost, to observe my behavior, but always under the lifelong excuse of looking elsewhere, of probing for the truth of things. I am always its object, but the moment I state this, I am lost and a wall of self-consciousness comes between me and who I think I am. I am always one remove from myself if I think it is me I'm taking into account. Only by ignoring myself does the double image of that natural self-consciousness about things refocus itself into only one person. The secret is that we can only observe one of ourselves at a time. When we observe others, we imagine we are absent and our vision clears.

An Empty Soup Bowl

He put an empty soup bowl in front of me then walked away. I thought it must have some allegorical significance. The highly polished porcelain gave a stronger impression to the lack of contents than their simple absence. Then the waiter came and filled it up, and the thought of allegory almost fled until I looked up and noticed he had filled the water glass just outside my reach. Sometimes things occur that don't add up to any strategy against you, any conspiracy, but in fact there is always a conspiracy just one arm's length away from what you pay people to do, or just one person from the ally that you've imagined you made. In fact, people are not watching out for you. It is the all-seeing eye of mental illness that perhaps realizes this too clearly, that has understood best the tragedy that nobody is really looking. Its invention of the eye is over this acute awareness.

Refills

Why I like refills is that I can store them up. It gives me the greatest satisfaction to know that I have something in reserve, that behind what I expend I am backed up. As a child being taken away, placed in a school, I remember a clear white plastic toy gun into which I could insert little colored balls of candy. And a refill I had. I remember how I fingered it on the long ride from my home. How it gave me a sense of security that I could store up so many pieces of candy in the gun as a kind of ammunition against being taken away, for the strange home I was being taken to. Not to shoot anybody of course, but as ammunition against them, nevertheless.

The Evening Clouds

The evening clouds blend with the mountains or look like they've been torn away, but never with a struggle. This is the way the impalpable should free itself from substance, painlessly, as if its separation is no more than a drifting. Who needs this tearing, renting, all the hue and cry of separation? It should be as little a marvel that things separate as they are together. We make too much of substance and its intangible precipitates, its exudates. We always demand a reason for sweating and think bodies must pay for it with chills. Rather bodies should melt down before the eye as effortlessly as clouds separate from mountains. They should be as willing to part with what adorns them, the moisture that accumulates on their crown, as these loftiest of mountains and remain standing mutely, without a word. No huffing and puffing, no sighs or groans. Then men would be equal to mountains.

What If You Had the Sensitivity?

What if you had the sensitivity to register every hurt you created in a woman? What if you--moderately attractive just by your mere being there, moving through the world --drew behind you a number of women, the way a ship would cause in its wake waves like furbelows or women's lace? But imagine that you had the leisure to notice every painful pattern of the lace. That you could stand on deck, that you, by the faculties awarded you, saw how each pattern formed trailing after you and fell back into the ocean hopeless of ever following. And it was no more than your mere presence, the encouragement your passage gave, the ship you were aboard, that the waves in your wake observed as the sleekness of your flanks--for invariably they told you they were attracted to thin men like yourself, or to the commanding position of your nose, the prominence of its bridge that seemed to cleave whatever element it carried you through with dispatch and certainty. Now imagine you knew of and felt all the things they admired in you, these lacy, frothy, furbeloved women, and you were in fact half-attracted to them; they gave your body buoyancy, indeed your very existence and support in life was because of them, because of the willingness of their bodies to submit to you and your kind (and without them you for sure would be lost). But you knew of the multiplicity of the demands they made on you, the deep, almost unbearable regret of their parting, the fact that you could take only so much of them aboard yourself, that you could only travel alone, though the waves licked at your bow, sprang up your sleek flanks, fell away in disappointment from you who seemed all steely and strong, who they imagined to be special, to rise out of the sea of their desires for. Imagine if you were standing on the aft one night and looking at them fall away from you, if you the evening being moist and a bit chill could taste the salt of what you imagined to be their tears, as they individuated themselves month by month all your life, climbed up your body, and you sunk deep and consciouslessly in theirs, imagine if you could enumerate them one by one that you couldn't live with yourself, that you became so overwhelmed by the passage of your little vessel that you imagined, while cleaving their bodies so easily to be impervious to them, to their entering you, imagine if you one day, standing on the aft, threw yourself overboard. You would find that none of them would want you, would recognize you; instead, you would find them pursuing the captainless ship until it too, from lack of direction, sank.

Her Cats

The cats seemed like the most stubborn and willful thin-lipped excuse not to give her feelings to people. People who had long since ceased to make demands on them. They now left her to her cats, and it was with them that she clearly wanted to be. But still, when she could hold one of them up and hug them, she always seemed to be doing it out of spite. That the way she drove her fingers into their fur squeezing them, only seemed to convey to you that the cat was a substitute. It was as if she bore the fear that if she didn't show you this openly, remind you of it, she might one moment--had her personality not been fixed, determined by so many years of cat loving--forget her cats. But the next you suspected she'd surely remember, not finding the people she had given herself to either furry or purring. She would quickly reach for the animals again.

The Donkey

It is the donkey in you that transports the burden of yourself through life. The braying recalcitrance that quickly gives you away even when you try to hide your ears with a hat, or not smile so much to show the size of your teeth, or drink little not to have the immoderate redness the nose is heir to attract attention. Still, it is the rocks on your back, the protuberant withers, the hindquarters that catch people's attention, that people, even blindfolded, are able to pin any tail they want on you.

The Cat Below My Window

The cat below my window has a housebroken meow. The black and white cat with a bell around his neck. He thinks he'll get his desire of the female by compromise, by talking things over so to speak. It's an illusion that comes from living with people too long. Instead of pouncing on her or giving his voice all that shrill freedom of a mock anger. That would give the slighter brown and white cat reason to submit, keeping her dignity. But this pleading that I hear, this milksop meow, no female cat with a shred of dignity would submit to that, not to mention the tinkle of the bell.

Donkey Ears

He collected donkey ears, he said, for all the times he'd acted the ass in life. He'd visit abattoirs and pay a nominal fee for them. Dry them in the sun on his balcony till the odor was almost gone, though admittedly he took a certain pleasure smelling the dry interiors and the way the fringe of hair tickled his nose. He then sewed them onto beanie hats so they flopped and could be donned the very instant he did something that made an ass out of himself. And the ears were disproportionately long, and their weight exceeded that of the cotton beanies, and so he was always losing them. That's why he said he had the almost full-time job of scouring abattoirs just trying to keep his hat on his head.

Callus

What if everything developed a callus? The lid you popped off thickened the thumb, the railing you held onto similarly thickened the palm? What if all these things thickened you so that you couldn't respond anymore? That finally, whatever you touched had been touched before, and that you lacked feeling through the callus. That the callus alone absorbed all sense of proximity with life. You would knock into things without knowing it. They would collide with you, but your callousness would protect you. Would this not be an ideal development? And is this not what happens?

A Thinning Principle

There's a thinning principle in myself that tries to live off the fat of what I think, an innate abundance that robs my body of the capacity to absorb from without. This is originality. What feeds off itself nourished by its own ideas, till it is a specter of a person. And it may have nothing to do with physical appearance, though this is perhaps the easiest sign. The person can't gain weight himself for fear that the moment of rest, contentment, physical acquirement, will somehow deprive his thoughts of impact, of body.

Something Clambering Up Your Face

Imagine if there was something always clambering up your face. But to keep your countenance you had to pretend that there was no scandent interference with what you looked like. Pretend to a smoothness that your face didn't have. Pretend that there was nothing to be held onto despite ears and a nose, despite enough length of hair that any number of things could pull themselves past the full and undeniable view of your eyes. Calmly, your look insists in all seriousness that your face can't be scaled. That nothing can climb it. Or that you have the mobile faculty of turning abruptly away if something suspects it has the capacity to. Of sneezing, coughing, wrinkling up your nose if some climber imagines he can get a hold on what you look like.

The Range of Personality

What if the range of personality were jagged like mountains, had its ups and downs, its peaks, its descents, its ravines and moraines? If the torsion took place in another era, and no matter what atmospheric experiences in one lifetime, it gave the impression of never being moved? And the mining that was done on the personality, even the spirited excavations, dented it no more than tin mining would change the conformation of the Andes. There is something about the personality determined by twisting, torsions, more heat than matter can bear, something determined that life itself--even lived passionately--is only the cool aftermath of.

The Clouds

Today the clouds are fluffy, easily dispersed by the sun. They have no resolve, but let the sun shine through, penetrate them. Would you call clouds immoral for this? And if a woman were just as fluffy and as easily--the day being similarly unparalleled blue--penetrated, why should she be called immoral? Why do we require her to grow cloudy, overcast, gloomily closed to what is no more than brightening sunlight? What would give her more radiance than the sun, more than can sometimes be looked at with the naked eye.

Dad Tickling Me

"It started with Dad tickling me," she said. "I had stayed back from school, I don't remember what for, but I was in my nightgown and Dad was partially dressed. We joked and were having such a good time. His holding me, tickling me, letting me go! I scampered free, let out explosions of laughter. And from him too, bursts of air as I wriggled in and out of his grasp. Then all of a sudden Mom returned and yelled at us. Scolded Dad and said, "I never want you to do that again." And he was so embarrassed. Right in front of me she scolded him. And his face got red as if he had done something that would never have crossed his mind had Mom not come home and yelled at him like that."

Cruelty

I wonder if we ourselves don't encourage the cruelty, the coldness of our loved ones, just to make our feelings for them more manageable. Who who truly loved could move with the magnitude of his feelings? Who, if they weren't periodically quartered by cruelty, drawn smaller by the lover's coldness, by some pettiness, could bear the sheer size of love? Love would become like an unsupportable tumor that would swell beyond the capacity of the body to carry it. The result of too much warmth would make what we feel for each other unmanageable. We have the best reasons in the world for our coldness, for what seems to be only our inhumanity. We are simply reducing the world to a size we can care for.

Family

A family is a handle on life. Knobs like breasts we first teethed on. Soon the knob grows smaller as our grip enlarges, and finally shrinks altogether. The door opens, often a thick door. There's creaking. But what we find is no person, no loving family, but only after all the embrace of nature. There are to be sure shadows, shades, scoldings, playful taunting, protestations of love. But behind the door is no more than the frame house. No matter how old the family, your birth into it is always a recent construction. And if you stay with it long enough-- despite your tergiversations, how much you ignore them, turn away, the house is only a bare frame after you open the door. And behind it nature, the surf, a grassy knoll at best. Some illusion of a body that will pillow you. Or is all this emptiness the result of having no sister? Or one that you never were sexually attracted to, or one that married and settled for someone else, left you alone. And as you stand looking from the threshold of the frame house, is it only the wizened hand of some parent you see for a moment expressing something, some sign from a wave about to crest, to break?

5

She Said She Wrote Me a Letter

She said she wrote me a letter on Sunday and mailed it Monday. And that there was a poem in it for me. I waited all week, and the next, and the next, trying not to jump to conclusions, trusting that even if she pasted on the incorrect postage (the rates had just changed) it would still get to me. I waited and hoped that if my world with her was tumbling, as always happened when she wouldn't see me for any length of time, I'd at least have the letter as evidence that she cared. Finally, the letter never came, and I realized that the poem she meant was that there wasn't a poem. But it was a poem too--for if by definition a poem elicits feeling, it fulfills itself. And my expectation of her letter for three weeks, expending every ounce of feeling every day, that was the poem (I finally realized) she must have meant. Every day that I listened for the postman's scooter to bring it, and the wheels died away like the end of lines trailing off to something inexplicable and suggestive, or every day I swung open the door quickly and tried to see a white letter on the floor through the dark. They were the poems she was giving me. And here, all along, I concluded that she hadn't written.

Sampaguitas

The sampaguitas you sent me were very nice. The inscription inside was beautiful. How did you ever think to select such a card? How thoughtful of you to have remembered my birthday. Are you that considerate about everything? If so, that augurs well for our future. Yes, I just lifted the card up in the air and let the bouquet catch the light--on my birthday--and thought how much you felt for me, and how wonderful it could have been if you had actually been here with me so I could thank you in person, and show you all my feelings, reciprocate your kindness, repay you for remembering my birthday. Before, or rather lately, my birthday has not been so important, but since knowing you, it has taken on an added significance, and all the delicious pleasure of half expecting you to write and now having your card in my hands, your well-wishing. Yes, your greetings to me, and yes, the sampaguitas, their fragrance, my lovely little Filipina, my beauty, I can all attribute it to you. And even though I have no milk white card to hold up in the morning light, to go with my memory of your beautiful brown skin, I do have the sampaguitas you represent--the flowers in my mind, and the spelling I was able to check from the glossary of Jose Rizal's *Noli Me Tangere* to give not only the correctness of my impression of your card and properly name its bouquet, but to give at least more illusion of reality to what I imagined you sent me, than if it had really arrived.

Sometimes I'm Afraid

Sometimes I'm afraid to do anything between the intervals of seeing you. I fear for myself, and all the fictitious dangers that might not allow that meeting. Sometimes you want something so badly, so deeply, that you place obstacles in the way of getting it--you imagine difficulties that are not there just to balance the improportion of your desires, to temporarily distract yourself from the real obstacles that might get in the way. It is as if such a large amount of desire, of need and expectation, can't exist alone, isolated, and unhindered, but that something must get in its way.

My Feelings for Her

My feelings for her had no more than that brief, stubborn, mucilaginous strength of say a just-pasted-on postage stamp that finding the envelope incorrectly addressed, we immediately pull off with no damage to either the stamp or the envelope, save that some of the stamp--a portion of its mucilage--may have lost some of its staying or sticking power, or cannot so easily, without the assistance of an external glue, be repasted elsewhere.

A Woman's Naked Back

There is something about the beauty of a woman's naked back that her turning towards you always disappoints, no matter who they are. The back, for the moment, has all the anonymity of your desire, that you don't have to pin it down with an identification. When we identify our desire with some person or other, it is always then turning into something else, losing its character, becoming compromised, and never again allowed its full and impersonal expression. A desire that stops, thinks about itself, i.e., considers the person it is drawn towards, turns self-conscious, benign, considerate, itself becomes faceless, something else besides desire.

What Frame of Mind Is She in?

"What frame of mind is she in?" Who can picture that? That leaping, bounding, gallery of moods that tries to put someone four-square between even the most ornate, gold-leafed carving. A mood if it is worth its salt would leave that in an instant. The frame of mind bordering only a shambles of thought that leaped from picture to picture to accommodate spectators, not so much for what it thought. A frame of mind then is nothing pictorial, in itself, but depends on the viewer, on who is coming, on whether the gallery is full or empty.

The Imperfections of Face

You pull her to you, past the imperfections of face, past the crookedness of the eyes, the weak lid so frail that the lashes seem like tiny arrows painful to look at, and the nose high and arched but obtruding into everyone's business, even your own. And the tiny scars on the cheek, and the chin willful, thrusting, and the mouth, the mouth all avarice when it smiles, all greedy lustful sexuality, the smallness of it, the abbreviated line, the thin lips, so ungenerous you wonder how they could be made for kissing. The whole face crooked, and there before you, how could she ever be drawn to the picture you have of yourself looking at her?

Teeth

His first thought was to check. Are they really her front teeth? Their evenness made him suspicious. The evenness he demanded, the proportion that would enable him to love her was also the basis for his deepest doubts. He remembered when they were out walking in the forest. "Oh, what teeth did the dentist work on?" he said nonchalantly. Actually, her answer was of dire interest to him. She showed him. "And which of the teeth are not real?" he asked. "Uh, this one right here, and this one," and she kept pointing around her mouth faster than he could calculate how many, what percentage of her teeth she was actually missing, before he could calibrate just what effect that would have on his own feelings for her. Was it forty percent that were missing, and which ones, yes, that was important. Were the front two teeth real? She didn't point to them. He was dying to ask her. Finally, unable to help himself he blurted out, "And what about these?" "Oh, the front ones?" She backed away as she pointed to them. "Oh, they're alright." But still, he had his suspicions. Still, they looked too straight for him. Then the incongruity of his questioning, his getting her to open her mouth--here in the forest with the tallest cedar trees all around, with the blanket of pine needles on the ground, and the sun sending a radiance of light on them--must have occurred to her, for she clamped her mouth shut like a vice and would answer no more questions. She, in a soft fox coat, and he, he still trying to get a look inside her mouth, trying to extract from her, the best he could, the truth about her missing teeth.

The Ugly Woman

The ugly woman across from me with three squirming children. I don't know whether to have sympathy or disgust for her. She is, at the moment, eating bread that is dropping from her mouth as she is paying half-attention to it. All the children now--in imitation of her--pull out boxes of food similarly making crumbs. They are all dressed in hats and pseudo-stylish clothes of one sort or another. It seems that all their squirming, discontent, irritability, stems from the large nose and stringy hair of the mother. That without those features on her face everyone would be sitting more calmly, content not to be looked at, or make a spectacle of what nature has misawarded the face of the mother. That fortunately hasn't been passed on to the children. It is that you want to look away that the mother gets your attention, her simple unattractiveness. Which wouldn't be a bad thing in itself. It is that she in her appearance rebels against her looks. That is what makes her noteworthy. That she doesn't accept what she looks like, and plunges her children with her in despair. How? By trying to draw as much attention as they can in public. By behaving as unsociable as possible. After all, she has been awarded a face that people might look away from. Chances are just ignore. But perhaps look away from. Any woman might be angry over that. Well, the first thing such a woman would do is attempt to make duplicates of that face, and when she couldn't do it even after two, three children simply make a spectacle of all of them in public. Draw people's attention. But the spectacle is not enough. For she has just slapped the younger child disproportionately hard. For almost doing nothing. It is with a strength that exceeds anything the child could do, or even has the body to accept. But it is her looks again. They are rebelling against what they look like, striking out even against the attractiveness she gave birth to. Maybe she thinks the slap will be hard enough that it will turn the child's head around so fast that she instead will look like him. Maybe somehow it is this impossibility that she is thinking of.

Busu

"*Busu*," she said, "do you know what that means?" To get a laugh. That was the catchword Japanese use. But it was a word that pulled out the stops, that determined me. All her beauty fell prey to that word. All that I had been avoiding, all that temporarily swayed me from my ends, all the humiliations I had absorbed, all these things broke open. She was the most beautiful woman I had seen circulating through Tokyo and Yokohama. I can't describe her beauty. The skin that surpassed mere covering. It was like some substance that seemed out of place. And the eyes the largest of their kind among her people; big and black with lids that curved like two dove's bodies. The beauty made me suspect that it was a mask of a face. That only now did the reference to the Japanese for "ugly woman" to get a laugh unmask.

The Dress

When she came out dressed, gowned for the autumn school gala in a rust brown, rusk orange dress--that she herself had made--that perfectly set off the browns, the smooth ruddy pigments of her complexion--when she came out to the dinner table around which were encircled all her relatives, and her father caught sight of her, I couldn't tell how the outraged sneer from somewhere deep in his gorge didn't suddenly pass through all the food he had been eating, and heave it on his daughter's dress, or just what gave the sneer sound, or if that did in fact precede the words of total disgust. "What's this, May?" he screamed at his wife. "What's this!" he screamed at his daughter as he kept pointing to the cleft in her dress, that though she didn't have much of a bosom, nevertheless dropped down to a precipitous V. "What's this?" he sneered, dessert dropping out of his mouth, as if the dining-room table were empty of guests. "What's this?" He jumped up and stuck his finger in the cleft and pulled at her dress. "Daddy!" his daughter now scolded as she pulled back and implored her mother. His finger pulling to give the utmost emphasis to just what he was talking about as his mouth twisted with the words, "She's not going out like that, May, did you know about that?" "What's wrong with it?" his wife asks. "Look at that," he said frothing at the mouth, his lips a white foam. "Just look at that. She's not going out like that," the spit now flying from his lips. The daughter started to cry before everyone who sat in silence. Her mother finally said, "OK, get a needle and thread and sew it up." "Can you imagine that? The kids today..." the father mumbled turning back to his dessert.

Character

What is character? Isn't it a stiff armor we put on our behavior to render it inflexible? So people get their wish of us, and we move less within it, never stray to those paths of behavior that they themselves have lacked the courage to wander? And so our curiosity goes into the armor, and the only movement it conveys is the squeaking of its joints as it bends to a pleasure that has left long before we can reach it.

6

Feeling Ebullient

Feeling ebullient the day I found I didn't have to pay the six hundred dollars income tax, I on my way home said to the Japanese teacher who had helped me translate my wage statement, "Do you have to go right home? I know a good baked rice restaurant that if you'll come, I'll pay." We went. After, at the cash register, I insisted on paying as I had said. When we got outside and were on our way to the bus stop, he said, "How about some coffee?" "No," I said, "I've had enough." (It is something of a Japanese custom to go to coffee shops after eating.) Then across the street he said again, "How about some coffee?" "No, I've had enough." "Come on," he said. And starts walking past the bus stop down the street, so that out of politeness I must keep up with him and convince him that I have had enough and prefer not to sit in a coffee shop. "No, really, I don't want to go." "But there's a coffee shop just up ahead," he points, keeping up his brisk pace, thinking that his own momentum would overcome any objection I might have. "No, really," I stop. "I've had enough. I'd rather just go home" (not being able to provide more of a reason for not sitting and drinking coffee). "Really?" he says. "Yes," I repeat. Finally convinced of the strength of my objection he says, "Okay, I'll pay next time."

Vincent

"Vincent, clean it up!" (A glass had been dropped at poolside.) "V-i-n-cent!" the man said. He was not (didn't seem) a relative, though he spoke so strongly he must have been an acquaintance of the family, or maybe he was only someone who knew Vincent's name. "Ask for a broom." "Ask who?" said Vincent. "Go over and ask for a broom!" "Ask who?" said Vincent (looking around). "Over there," the man half-pointed (but without conviction as it seemed shouting at Vincent seemed more important). There were some waitresses around. One seemed to have disappeared for a broom. "You dropped it, Vincent, so you must clean it up!" "Yes, that's right, Vincent, it's your mess," someone else (another guest) chimed in. Vincent began to walk away, but the man's voice again drew him back to the broken glass. "Vincent!" he said threateningly. "I don't want to clean it up," Vincent simpered. "Vincent!" the voice boomed around the pool and out onto the lawn of sunbathers. "Poor Vincent," someone half-muttered. The girl came with the broom. "No," the man said, "let Vincent clean it up." "I don't want to," he said still trying to walk away. "You knocked it over, Vincent," he echoed to the girl already sweeping. All I could conclude from this was that of all the people that afternoon around the pool, not one of them would ever choose the name Vincent for their son.

The Piano Player

At first, when the piano player stopped in the middle of his performance and left the stage, the concert managers were appalled and quickly vowed that never again would he play in another hall. But what they found among the theater goers was an enchantment with the piano player. His stopping unexpectedly captured their imagination. Various and sundry speculations circulated, rumors explaining the player's actions. Some whispered that he had a secret lover, that he was fulfilling some sort of promise to her. Others speculated that perhaps the burden of his gifts climaxed that night and he yielded to their weight. Nevertheless, they clamored for his reappearance the more stubborn were the theater personnel. Finally, they submitted to the demands of the public. Audiences flocked to his recitals in anticipation of a repeat performance of what by now had become legendary. Each time the audience sat on the edge of their seats savoring every moment they felt the piano player might stop and leave the stage. The suspense of this is what they came for, was the reason why the piano player developed such a wide following. Not so much to hear the piano player play, but to wait for him to stop. They hung onto every movement in anticipation of this with a pleasure that never before did the music bring. The wave of it that crested somewhere through his performance--crescendoed when he reached the highest notes and ended in a pianissimo, the softest acquiescence that whispered, no, this was not yet the night. Still the audience left each performance with the feeling that indeed they had gotten their money's worth for the repeat performance this one led up to.

Sumo

There was a fire in the sumo arena on the last day of the tournament. Choking with fans. Someone yelled "fire," and indeed smoke arose from somewhere. But it was the wrestlers at the periphery when they weren't performing on the center ring who were first to the exits. (Despite the customary ritual of the sumo world, they had no rites of passage out of the arena in the event of a fire.) As the wrestlers exited in each case almost two by two, they stuck in the doorways. And not their most graceful movements on center ring, nor the best techniques they used with their opponents, enabled them to give an inch and unwedge their huge bodies that the very anxiety to escape from the smoking arena only jammed tighter. The spectators fanned out only to find their heroes hopelessly wedged against the exits, holding the crowd back. Finally, the most avid of Tokyo fans were consumed by the same ardor that drove them to the arena in the first place, but that now would not let them leave.

Grandmother

Miss Ito takes care of her grandmother who is half-paralyzed. She doesn't mind because as she reasons, she was taken care of by her as a child. She remarks: "When she bathes, she needs my great help. I don't mind helping her, though it is not so easy as her taking care of me when I was a baby."

"Thanks child, the water feels so comfortable on my aches."
"I'm glad, grandmother." Because of you I can't be with him tonight. Every night I must bathe and massage you--your aches. Grandmother, I am tired. Grandmother, I'm getting old. "I'm getting old child, I'm not as young as I once was." My skin is getting dry bathing you, grandmother; my hands are wrinkled and shrinking--I'm afraid that he will soon think them too small to hold. And my skin is being rubbed away massaging you, grandmother, my fingertips are losing their feeling. I'm afraid they will be unfit to touch him. "Oh, that feels so good." And the steam of the bathwater is drying out the oils in my hair--it is losing its gloss--its luster. Oh, grandmother, I'm afraid. "That's right child, your fingers are so long and supple, better than any comb on my scalp. What would I do without you? I have always needed you, my little one. Even when you were a baby, I needed you. He was worthless, a good-for-nothing. You were such a gift." Oh, grandmother, my arms are aching. "I can feel your strength in your fingers, they are taking my aches away. I feel strong for you child, young again!" Oh, God, help me. "What did you say, child? You are so devoted. An angel. But

104

why are you so silent? I know you must be getting weary of your old grandmother. Child, say something. What is it? Child, why are you pressing my shoulders like that? Child, stop, stop. Ch…"

Hiromi

Hiromi didn't like raisins. That's the result of being your Daddy's favorite, I told her, of being his only daughter. His feelings for you were as refined as your picking out the raisins in everything. They were as broad-palmed in pulling you smotheringly towards him, rubbing you with his beard and hot breath, as years later twisting your face up in disapproval towards the raisins continued to be the sharp reproof you didn't have the strength for--your father enormous shouldered, and with splay hands that could enwrap your whole head--instead what you did periodically was take a half step back, contort your face in disgust, pinch your thumb and index finger together, and pick out the raisins from the shortcake, the ice cream, the cereal, signaling a disapproval that you could never show towards his hot embrace, but that the raisin was the perfect substitute, fitting as it did between the soft pads of your fingers, and not making a murmur of resistance even when it was the eyes of a gingerbread man you removed them from.

Half a Head of Hair

In Japan the high school girl has less than half a head of hair. The rest seems to have fallen out. It is an uneven stubble where the white scalp shows through at places. The swath of healthy hair is long and black. This is the portion that her friend accompanying her doesn't identify with. From the determined, stubborn, almost defiant look on her face, you can quickly tell her presence is purely based on the absent hair and accounts for the scornful looks she gives on the bus, even in the absence of classmates that might be openly critical.

Same

We get up together, eat the same oatmeal, eggs, toast, drink the same coffee and orange juice, read the same morning paper, take the same walk, sit down at our desks at the same time. Eat the same salad and soup for lunch. Do the same dishes, and shop at the same supermarket, prepare the same supper together, chicken, rice, and broccoli; share the same ice cream for dessert over a sliced banana with a dash of brandy. We listen to the same radio programs after doing the same dishes and sharing the same opinions. At the same time, we brush our teeth, and wash up at the same sink, and at eleven o'clock we get into the same bed, and caress each the same body, and finally drift off to a different sleep.

One Day in the Philippines

One day in the hot Philippines, when everyone else stood in the shade, he walked across the street from the small bus station and stood in the afternoon sun. He stood there under the beating sun and watched the people he had stood with a moment before, watched them as the sweat poured out of him, as the sun beat down on him. His forehead grew redder and redder, like a lobster of which the dazzling sun was the pincers. He swayed and then a curious thing happened. All at once he stopped sweating, and the sun left a nimbus of light around him; where before it had been reflecting and his eyebrows glistened, now the man was conspicuous by his dryness, now the red forehead didn't seem an isolated instance of sunburn, of beating heat, but blended with the colors of the sun, intermingled with their dazzling. And a curious thing then happened to the people watching this man with the high exposed forehead, transfigured before their eyes; they who had actually irrespective of the shade they stood in achieved a kind of coolness from watching the sweating man suffering in the sun. His motive cannot be fully ascertained, though its effect on the observers was clear enough. Perhaps it was the simple desire to elevate himself from the people he was standing with, or to free himself from waiting; perhaps it was a simple martyring impulse, his desire to cool them; perhaps it was the sun that drew him on. In any event what happened now to the dazzling figure in the mid-afternoon sun was that he made the people standing in the shade, for whom he had served as an example of their own coolness, a living, sweating example of just how comfortable they were, begin to sweat (right there in the shade) more and more profusely until finally, all at once, by some strange collective impulse, they crossed the street and gathered round him. Without looking at him, but with eyes looking straight ahead as if they had no intention of getting the bus. In fact the bus came and stopped, but the people surrounding the dazzling man in white didn't move. Their own multi-colored outfits as if formed the spectrum of his, his being the prism of theirs because of his refractive capabilities, because of the way he managed the sunlight. Slowly, the bus pulled away, but the people were as immobile as the man in white led them to be. By nightfall, and the time of the next bus, the man in white was dead. The people had collapsed around him and had to be carried away on stretchers. But since that time people come daily from distant provinces to stand in the sun every afternoon, out of homage to the man in white. They have long forgotten the perspiration that appeared under his armpits, and never mention how it soaked through his clothes. They now insist that he never perspired.

7

The Carpentiers

It is fascinating how the mind can temporarily obey the fact that what you know allows itself to be nullified by what you don't know; both facts are suspended in a limbo until the one punches free, and you recall the other and then think, *Oh, yes, they have the same name.* You knew both, but never made the connection, for the one eclipsed the knowledge of the other. For example, I look up in a 1950 Concise Encyclopedia to see if Alejo Carpentier is listed. Instead, I find the boxer, Georges Carpentier, and think, *Is the Cuban born writer's name in fact spelled differently?* But then I find that, no, they are the same. The fighter and the writer who I never associated before. Both Carpentiers, both master workmen of their respective trades. The poetry of the one can be captured by the other. The clear-mindedness of the one will triumph over the punch-drunkenness of the other as through the maze of so many punches thrown, so many jabs absorbed, so many rounds. Already I can see the writer in the audience capturing it all and relate both names in a way that the enforced grogginess of my own mind would never have dreamed of had I not one day decided to look up Alejo Carpentier, and found Georges.

Francis

What cancels memory without our knowing it are similarities that cross temporarily, inhibiting the passage of information. Your uncle, e.g., is named Francis. The little boy whose name you can't think of when one day he locked himself in the bathroom is also called Francis. Your uncle has made a deep impression on you, and you've always liked the little boy. Your uncle has been in a mental hospital the last fifty years. Francis, being nine or ten, has his whole life ahead of him. Your mind fails to connect the two, jams the passage of names just like the lock little Francis is unable to open--like the hospitalized mind too that isn't forthcoming. Maybe it needs oiled by the possibilities of the little boy, to lubricate the admission of your uncle who has spent his whole life under lock and key.

When Your Mood Is Destructive

There are moments when your mood is destructive; it is bent on vengeance (that may be no more than a spasm of material discontent with the substance at hand)--that you are unwilling to take the time necessary to follow to its origin. It is just that you want to break something (the main thing), alter what you would normally have patience with. Smash it--you lunge this way and that, tearing, bumping, hurling what you have in your hands against the wall or into the sink, and are only half-careful that if it is glass it doesn't shatter near your eyes. We are on the precipice of harming ourselves and naively claim because the world is in the way. I used to think it was from a kind of sexual frustration, but I've learned that it is more than that, something antidotal to the greatest care we take with ourselves, something that perhaps punishes us for not being blind enough to our interests, that gets tired with whom we watch out for, something trying to be more impersonal than we are accustomed to being with ourselves. Something we usually require of other people. But when we are solitary, or have learned from experience well enough not to let them hurt us, it is ourselves that we must rely on to do the damage that our wellbeing, that our looking too much out for ourselves, foments.

Rock Candy

One day fifteen years later, you are standing before a class of Japanese students. The women all dressed to the T, some in the latest fashions, buttoned at the neck, arms crossed or folded on their desks, and you think of her. How you both had no money the day you drove her to Fisherman's Wharf for a job interview. And when she came back, she said, "He asked me to take my top off." What!" you said. "To see if I would do it, and could model some of their new lines. He said he owned two stores in San Francisco." "And only your top?" you asked. "No," she said. "And did you do it?" She didn't answer. You're angry now: "Did you?" "Yes," she answered curtly and embarrassed. "Let's get some rock candy," you say to your class forgetting for a moment where you are. "I mean, Miss Watanabe, if you can't see the print, don't you have glasses?" "Oh, yes," she puts them on as a hard brilliance catches them with a crystalline light that your memory devours as something almost sweet.

A Split Mind Is Convenient to Hide the Axe

Nobody will identify the glitter of the buried axe in the darkness of the split mind. Nobody ever sees it wielded in the sunlight again. Instead, the split mind sheathes it completely. Never mind the calluses on the hands of those who swing it, the hostility of wood in even feminine hands. And when medication makes the split mind lose control of the facial muscles, the family is as far from blaming the sharp blade embedded in the mind as they are from accounting for the disappearance of the calluses on their own hands.

The Aberrations of His Friends' Backgrounds

The aberrations of his friends' backgrounds had always been a badge of distinction for him. The fact that one friend's father bludgeoned his mother to death with a lead pipe while he sat in the highchair watching; that the other friend's parents committed suicide separately. He was proud of these things as if they had happened in his own family. Perhaps only if they had, would he have been ashamed.

The Hernia

In the dark of his room, in the secret of his body, was the hernia. Later we learned some vague strangulation had taken place, pushed through consciousness into the lower intestine, the lumen, cavity, the space inside his body that determined the free play of our imagination. Was it the vague fears that we'd be found out as the reason for the operation? Our own periodic surgery on his body, the wielding of the most precise instruments of pleasure, the facial features that we balanced encouraging him against the shame. His eyes watering to hide the body, our mouths taking a twisted pleasure in what he was doing to himself in front of us, and how he wouldn't look at himself during the sessions, bore analogy to the mystery now surrounding him. That we all felt partially responsible for the hernia that we didn't understand--hidden as it was in the dark recess of a body--that this time we didn't have access to, but that somehow still seemed to go with his chicken chest.

VD

The day X caught VD he limped into the dining room. Dishes scattered, people rushed for the exits ("VD, VD!" they shouted.). The cutlery twisted like corkscrews, spirochetes he imagined coursing through his bloodstream, rushing for the organs. X imagined all this, of course, for everyone was sitting calmly finishing their supper. The VD was not in his bloodstream but only in his brain, in that advanced stage of his thinking about it.

Lentils

My apartment tonight smells of lentils—the peasant's dish. Cheerless, gloomy, mouse brown, grayish lentils that smack of saving money, of trying to make ends meet. How can I expect a knock on the door when I cook lentils and add celery and onions? A knock on the door as the pot bubbles and my eyes water? A knock on the door as I cut up a fresh tomato to give taste? A knock on the door after I've eaten alone, imagining the double convexity of someone there bedside me, or a lens that I can hold up to focus on a person in the distance? My apartment is perched on a hill, a Mt. Palomar that will reach out through the stars traveling at such speeds as desires do when the apartment is smelling of cooked lentils, and one of them still has enough shape to make a lens that will span galaxies looking for the woman who has not knocked yet, and probably never will.

Meaning

There is a sense that we want to hide meaning once we've uncovered it. Life can't exist on too much meaning, or--and maybe this is the key--any meaning at all for long. There is no oxygen, no breath to be gotten from meaning. This is why people--even those dedicated to pursuing it--uncover it only on occasion and are never able or willing to sustain it, that they quickly lose and often on purpose the meaning they've found.

Politics

A true artist worth his salt always has half an eye on politics. The government he is not a part of. The unpoetry of it. The irrelevance of his own abilities. The deep desire to be like Christ, and enter the temple, and upset the merchants' tables. Even those that sell doves. Christ had no patience with the peacemakers. Blessed they are when he is legislator. But the moment he becomes unacknowledged, even their tables are overturned.

8

Vermont Winter

Driving through the Vermont winter, white, white snow all around. And the black, black bark of trees. The contrast goes deep inside. The black trees, the white snow. The branches reaching out stiff and creaking, I can hear the limbs when I stop. My breath I can see, the life is still there. My nose begins to lose sensation, grow numb, my fingers, too. The white snow all around harkens, pulls, drags me back down Interstate 91, down I-95, down to the Cross Bronx Expressway exiting at Jerome Avenue, back ten winters ago. As frigid as Vermont that night under the el. It is past midnight, two or three in the morning. A thick blanket of snow covers everything, the roads are iced. I am taking my taxi in having pressed my luck already and not gotten stuck. My garage is only a few blocks ahead. At a red light there is a knocking on my cab window. An old black couple asks, "Can I take them over the Concourse?" "No, I can't make it," I say, "up the hill." They plead with me. "No, I have no snow tires," and left them in the dead of night as immobile as the trees I now see every winter in Vermont, squeaking in the frigid temperatures. Each black bough, each dark trunk brings back their overcoats, dots the landscape with the appearance of reaching out stiffly frozen, barely able to move like the couple that walked away ever so slowly from my yellow cab--yellow as the sun, yellow as a wheat field in autumn, yellow as the butter that I melted on the French toast I stuffed myself with at breakfast the next morning.

Imaginary Dresses

Imaginary dresses tear loose from the blades, screams pierce the air, the flutter of blinding white undergarments in the sunlight exposes bare arms, tumbled bodies, entangling with the powerful grip of workmen on the Vermont highway crew that have just stormed in broad daylight a castle, and ravished the ladies-in-waiting as they cut down one Queen Anne's lace after another leaving the roadway strewn with apparel and naked limbs, as smooth as the sunlight reflecting off their tools. Finally, they wave me on to pass in silence the carnage.

Irving

I remember her saying to him, "Irving, if you don't stop talking to yourself, the men in the white coats and butterfly nets are going to come and take you away to 11th and McClay." Chances are Irving was really talking with himself, but it is also possible that he was muttering some disapproval under his breath. In fact, she was the one who named Irving "the pack rat" because he hoarded things. First, he carried them in his bulging pockets, then deposited them in secret stashes, which when she uncovered them--calling all twenty-one of us to the basement--she would display smack in the middle of the dressing room floor. Our eyes all wide and her lip curling up to her nose in disapproval of old foodstuffs Irving had saved, or unlaundered socks she might find. The mentality was the opposite of finding a buried treasure. For Irving seemed to hide just what seemed most worthless. She, in one smooth motion, spilled it out from the shirts and socks he had them wrapped in, trifles we sometimes had discarded. But when we saw them strewn on the floor, the fruit of her uncovery, they would take on a value they hadn't had before, and we would be prompted to join her in accusing Irving of stealing what we had discarded. Perhaps Irving never knew the difference. For he, through this ritual of uncovering, when his soul was as if emptied of its contents there on the basement floor, would not utter a word of self-defense. His face would be that glowing pink that contrasted so well with his sparse wisps of blond hair. A uniform pink that told of his over-weight and the readiness of his blood to respond to any embarrassment. It was a sight there, all the hoardings spilled on the floor with Mrs. Shank yelling in Irving's face, "Pack rat, pack rat!" And the rest of us repeating the litany in chorus, "Pack rat, pack rat." And Irving just standing there stiffly under the bare basement light bulb in the center of the floor. His possessions at his feet, scattered all around the drain cover. His metal-rimmed glasses, because of the straightness of his posture, catching the light, blinding us of any chance to look into his eyes for an idea of what he was thinking. "Pack rat, pack rat," we chanted. And I remember her yelling, as she rooted through his things, for him to empty his pockets "right here and now, Mr. Provost!" Trying to erase even the dignity that his last name suggested.

Rebel

They called him "Rebel." He never lost a match in high school. Calm, cool, nobody could match him. No fire, even purposely extinguished. There was not even the suggestion of being on a low burn, of smoldering. The suggestion was that inside he was as glacial as his steel gray eyes were outside. His moves were textbook smooth, sharp and cutting to perfection. Like a jeweler's. As if there were some gem his body was cutting in the shape of his opponent. No room even for the athlete. Rather the perfected, oiled machine. His opponents on the mat knew that they had more than just a person they were dealing with. No warmth was to be expected. Our coach would tell tales of him. The most human was how before one big match, Rebel sat in the locker room and made a hangman's noose of the string on the hood of his uniform. And the way he dangled it before the match. He was the executioner. Cold, heartless. Unwary of any wrong that had been done. Just carrying out the dictates of his ability. He went to Oklahoma. But after a year, he dropped out, floundered, married, finally took to wearing suits, ties choking right up to his Adam's apple, representing the high school establishment he had represented on the mat. Went to a small local college, got his degree. Took to coaching the wrestling team for a few years, but though he was a natural winner, his kids weren't. (Some said he was too aloof. Couldn't come down to their level.) So, he dropped it. Remained distant to all but the confederacy of fans that worked him back into the establishment. He rose up in the Alumni Association, even became a perennial candidate for President. Every year he became more formal, more stiff. And when someone would call across the dance floor at its annual gathering, "Hey, Rebel," soon it began to sound odd. As if somewhere after graduation, after high school, he had lost, that winning so decisively, going against the grain, had swirled around and absorbed his knotty, wooden resistance, the high point in his life, absorbed it into the mainstream. So that now, in short, he was no longer a rebel.

The Balding Athlete

His body bears the remnants of battle, the trick knee, the cauliflower ear, the bone chips at the elbow. Every night in his sleep he tosses and turns on the mat, holding his opponent, bridging, twisting, throwing half-nelsons and chicken wings. But in the end, his wife slips out of them all to wake him before she's smothered in another victory that he feels compelled to wrest from the jaws of defeat in the final moments of a troubled sleep. "Always before the bell, always before the bell!" he complains she wakes him. That this time he would have won, had time not run out.

Boxes

Her apartment was so cluttered--the cardboard boxes went up to the ceiling. On each were pasted their contents: "Newspaper Clippings, must go through," "Pictures, must draw," "Photographs, must sort," "Art Books," "Poetry," "Lace Blouses," "Braids of Hair." More labels than you would have imagined a person had boxes for. But in a two-room apartment they all fit somehow. Amongst them all her emotional life was distributed. They went back to the 1930s when she first started to live alone. There was a time when in the late 1940s and 1950s she seemed to have found herself, when there were possibilities. When her apartment still had space. When there weren't so many boxes yet. When there was still one wall free. There was hope then. She was painting the murals that extended the length of her wall. That she unrolled for visitors. She still thought she would go somewhere. Find her place in the art world. In fact, she was taking courses at the Fashion Institute. She did then large wall paintings of the city at night. Of the buildings out her fire escape window glowing with little golden rectangles of light. From her apartment it seemed she was able to capture all the warmth spilling out of the city windows. And in winter she was able to add those dusk purples that went so well with the gold of the electric lights. With the otherwise bulky apartment buildings, that she made so delicate, depicting the windows as she did. Gradually, however, her coursework at the Fashion Institute snuffed out the creative freedom of her early introductory art courses. She became less inventive, more design, pattern conscious. She no longer painted the city at night, no longer captured the warmth in apartment buildings. The boxes grew and she complained to friends that she had no more space. Sometimes she dreamed and said, "I'd like to get my own studio, one room where I can work, where I won't be interrupted by my boxes." In the early 1960s, seeing her art career was going nowhere, she made a last-ditch effort at creativity. She was too old for breaking into the fashion industry. "They want young people," she would say with a sigh. And so, she took to painting her bathroom. She painted it pink, and on the walls she painted black flamingos and palm trees. She had always wanted to move to Puerto Rico, she said. Gradually, however, the flamingos lost their plumage, the paint peeled, their feathers molted, the palm trees dropped their coconuts on the tile floor.

Nevertheless, the boxes continued. Her art stopped altogether. Except for an occasional Christmas card. "I can't work in this apartment," she says. "There's no room." "Well, throw out your boxes," friends advise. "No, I must go through them," she replies. "To see what I have. I don't want to throw out anything valuable." Finally, her friends stop visiting, there being no room for them. And now she herself can only get into her bedroom walking sideways.

At the Louvre

It must be universal, or is there something spiteful only in a handful of us? The enormous tension of being around virtually priceless paintings and being able at one stroke to destroy an eye, dislodge a breast, drive a curl back into place, lop off toes, truly make of the sunflower a bull's-eye. All the power of this is overwhelming, and the cold eye of the security guard (almost an inducement in itself) knows it; it for certain inspires in him an electrical resentment of your being too close, or in the museum at all. You who are more affected by beauty than by life. The beauty that renders you limp, deprives you of all volition, takes the color out of your cheeks, the blue from your eye, weakens the chestnut browns in your hair (each painting turns it more gray), leaves you larval almost, a mere grub wriggling eyeless in amazement. It is little wonder that you stiffen in resentment, are metamorphosed in an instant, go hard, obtected as a chrysalis immobile there on the gallery floor that the guard soon loses interest in you, your circling back so often, till gradually you are reborn in a sudden outburst of resentment at being a mere insect before such beauty that overshadows you, that leaves you with no resource but to hide yourself under the nearest rock, in the bark of some tree, all the while you are standing there on the gallery floor. And then the next moment, squirming again at the beauty before you, pupa that you are, imago almost, you twist free of the influence of art, begin to pant and imagine on your own back wings that will in an instant carry you to the painting, that your hand will erase the most delicate part of a woman like a claw hammer, uncrown

Napoleon, take off Liberty's breast, the Odalisque's diadem, Dürer's left eye, you triumphantly reach through the guard's cold stare up through the snow of the Emperor in exile, unhat him, dislodge his tricorn with your five fingers, or attack Ingres's bottom digging into the soft flesh hoping she'll turn full towards you, uncouch herself. But your wings fail, the impulse crumples stillborn. You walk away and only write this.

In the Bar

Every detour he makes, every hesitation even at a stoplight, every suggestion tendered, every movement that you think is disinterested, is to fill the keg of his stomach with beer. To drain what sits in every bar, pub, saloon. He's game for them all. And his pool eye, his shuffleboard gaze, the pinball lights that dance and flicker, the sharp tip of each dart, all depend on tapping the keg. "Draft," he says in manly tones that all the customers can hear. And he nurses each drink just long enough to run the table, or till his bull's-eye is put out by the last fletched orange and blue dart. He knows how much alcohol it takes to light up the woman's breasts on the pinball machine, what straight shot will make her pink panties glow. The keg his stomach is, replaces that sitting behind every bar with a liquor license. And every two days he is drawn there to drain their contents through a maze of the most colorful games; the high balls on the green baize table he sinks one after the other into the pocket with the deftness of alcohol running through the conduits of his circulatory system, flushing out all memories that don't pertain to the game at hand. It is for that that he has developed the softest shot in the bar, and why he rarely loses.

9

Burnt Out

"I'm burnt out," she said suddenly to my surprise. She had come all the way to Tokyo to sing, and I had heard her performance given with feeling, straining her vocal cords to the limit, and now this simple admission after so many years. How could it be? Were there ashes in her mouth? Did they come from breathing acetylene out her nostrils? Was the singing now only screams of second-degree burns? Is that what she meant saying she was burnt out? Were there blisters on the skin, a charred body, a face, a voice unrecognizable? Burnt out! She doesn't know what it means.

Signs of Yellow

He checks his sputum throughout the day for turbidity, for signs of yellow. Anything craven, cowardly, he dissolves. Any quick movement of the head he quickly investigates its origin to ensure his not finding the chicken in himself. He is forever in the mirror trying to separate the sunlight on his back from every imagined yellow streak.

Know Thyself

Nature develops seasons to keep from boring herself. It is curious how it is indifferent to itself every moment, that it never stops changing. We, too, change for a reason. We want to remain interesting to ourselves--we want not to get to know ourselves. The opposite of what people think or say. To know themselves better. Maybe we need the dictum "Know thyself" because of the strength of our propensity not to. That, without that dictum, we would know nothing.

The People You Show You've Made It

The people you show that you've made it look at you stunned, realizing at that instant that that was the object of squandering all the years you could have had with them--just to make them proud of you, you broke off contact and now return with all the empty years in hand, in the form of a book that most probably catalogues all the times you wanted to return, but instead transformed into fiction it's almost certain they will never read.

Van Gogh's Chair

In Amsterdam a chair is trying to wash ashore, but its legs, keeping it from being so, make me think of Van Gogh's chair and the difficulty it had before the tide of opinion beached it high and dry on a museum wall.

Birds in Cages

The brilliant colors of the birds in cages in Mexico--the deep vermilions, luminous blues, greens, and purples, the orange, the yellow beaks with black bands, the indigo eyebrows--all haunt you for not buying one and setting it free. Something remains caged in you for having thought to yourself, it will just be caught again.

The Bat

His statement in the kitchen, when we suddenly turned on the light, that the bat "is more afraid of us than we are of it," sticks with me, and occasionally flies at me blindly, dives low and causes me to hunch my shoulders, almost duck, not so much at the memory of the bat, as the cliché I still can't get out of my mind.

Every Movement of the Gills

Imagine every movement of the gills a small explosion. Imagine if life breathing underwater bore analogies with the studied procedure of demolitions experts themselves blowing things up, and if every movement underwater was not something like overcoming the gunpowder to advance the body through life at a more rapid pace than the marine environment allowed. And so smoothly that the demolition was measured to the extent that pieces of gills, teeth, bone, scales were not flying haphazard through the air, but coasting through water more smoothly than were no explosive devices set off.

About the Author

Richard Krause has had three collections of fiction published titled *Studies in Insignificance* (Livingston Press*), The Horror of the Ordinary* (Unsolicited Press), and *Crawl Space & Other Stories of Limited Maneuverability* (Unsolicited Press). He also has had three collections of epigrams published, *Optical Biases* (EyeCorner Press in Denmark), *Eye Exams* (Propertius Press), and *Blind Insights into the Writing Process* (Fomite Press). Krause lived for nine years in Japan and drove a taxi for five years in NYC. He currently lives in Kentucky where he is retired from teaching at a community college.

About the Press

Unsolicited Press is based out of Portland, Oregon and focuses on the works of the unsung and underrepresented. As a womxn–owned, all–volunteer small publisher that doesn't worry about profits as much as championing exceptional literature, we have the privilege of partnering with authors skirting the fringes of the lit world. We've worked with emerging and award–winning authors such as Shann Ray, Amy Shimshon–Santo, Brook Bhagat, Kris Amos, and John W. Bateman.

Learn more at Unsolicitedpress.com. Find us on Twitter and Instagram at @UnsolicitedP.